SALAD AND VEGETABLE COOKING

Edited by Jane Solmson

WEATHERVANE
BOOKS

Contents

Introduction

Salads and vegetables don't have to be unimaginative back-burner dishes used to fill in the gaps of your exciting entrees. This full-color cookbook shows you how they can be main dishes, side dishes, only dishes; how they can add color, flavor, variety and nutrition.

On these pages are recipes for salads of every kind. Use salads of fruits, eggs and vegetables with spicy dressings to perk up warm weather meals. And special occasions deserve the rich taste of seafood or meat salads topped off with creative salad molds for attractive desserts.

Even more variety is to be found in the vast number of vegetables. Many cooks overlook the interesting textures and colors vegetables have to offer, usually with few calories and low cost.

To follow is a guide to these natural delicacies. From asparagus, beans, beets, and broccoli; carrots, cabbage, eggplant, and okra; to ways of preparing tomatoes, turnips, and zucchini that even Mother Nature hasn't thought of yet. Be creative and enjoy!

SALADS

chef's salad

2 cups cooked meat,
strips or flakes
1½ quarts lettuce, in
bite size pieces
½ cup chopped celery
1 tomato, cut in wedges
2 green onions, chopped

¼ cup green pepper, cut
in strips
3 hard-cooked eggs,
chopped
¼ teaspoon salt
⅓ cup French dressing

Combine ingredients; toss gently to mix. Serves 6.

notes

Use pork, ham, beef, veal, chicken, turkey, or tuna.

If preferred, replace half the lettuce with a mixture of other salad greens.

Use prechilled ingredients and a prechilled bowl for a crisp salad.

variation

Cheese or cottage cheese chef's salad. Use 1 cup cheese strips or 1 cup cottage cheese in place of 1 cup cooked meat.

pear and grape salad

4 ripe dessert pears
1 cup cream cheese
1-2 tablespoons French
dressing

½ pound black grapes
Crisp lettuce

Peel pears, cut in half. Scoop out core with a teaspoon.

Blend cream cheese with enough French dressing to make it spreadable; coat rounded side of each pear half.

Halve and seed grapes; press them into cheese, close together so that each pear resembles a small bunch of grapes.

Serve on crisp lettuce leaves. Serves 4.

fruit salad with nuts

1 small honeydew melon
2 oranges
1 cup blue grapes
Lettuce leaves
12 walnut halves

dressing
1 8-ounce container
  yogurt
1 tablespoon lemon
  juice
1 tablespoon orange
  juice
1 tablespoon tomato
  catsup
2 tablespoons
  evaporated skim milk
Dash of salt
Dash of white pepper

fruit salad with nuts

Scoop out melon with melon baller. Cut peel from oranges, remove white membrane; slice crosswise. Cut grapes in half; remove seeds. Line a glass bowl with lettuce leaves; arrange melon balls, orange slices, grapes, and walnuts in layers on top of lettuce.

Mix and blend well all ingredients for dressing. Adjust seasonings. Pour dressing over fruit. Let salad ingredients marinate 30 minutes. Toss salad just before serving. Serves 4 to 6.

japanese egg salad

7½ ounces canned tuna
  fish
1 can mandarin oranges,
  approximately 11
  ounces
16 stuffed olives
4 hard-boiled eggs

salad dressing
2 tablespoons oil
2 scant tablespoons
  lemon juice
2 tablespoons soy sauce
Salt
Pepper
Pinch of sugar
Parsley sprigs for
  garnish

Drain tuna fish; tear into bite-size pieces with a fork.

Drain mandarin oranges and olives. Slice olives and hard-boiled eggs. Toss all ingredients lightly.

To prepare dressing, combine oil, lemon juice, soy sauce, salt, pepper, and sugar; stir until well-blended.

Pour dressing over salad. Refrigerate for 10 minutes or longer. Divide among 4 individual glass bowls and garnish with parsley sprigs. Serves 4.

egg salad

1 package frozen peas
¼ pound crab meat
6 hard-cooked eggs
¼ pound smoked salmon

marinade
2 tablespoons
  mayonnaise
½ cup sour cream
1 teaspoon salt

Dash of pepper
1 teaspoon sugar
1 teaspoon lemon juice
½ bunch parsley

Cook frozen peas according to package directions. Cool; drain. Drain crab meat. Shell eggs; cut in small pieces. Cut smoked salmon in strips. Mix all ingredients carefully.

Mix mayonnaise and sour cream until lightly foamy. Add the rest of seasonings and chopped parsley. Pour marinade over salad, mixing gently. Refrigerate salad 10 to 15 minutes.

Garnish with tomatoes and parsley; serve. Serves 6.

cauliflower and avocado salad

1 medium size
  cauliflower
½ cup French dressing
1 ripe avocado pear
½ cup sliced stuffed
  olives

2-3 tomatoes, peeled
  and cut into eighths
½ cup crumbled cheese
  (Roquefort or bleu)
Lettuce or endive

Divide cauliflower into florets, cover with iced water; chill 1 hour.

Drain and dry cauliflower; chop coarsely. Put into a bowl. Pour over French dressing; leave for 2 hours.

Just before serving, add peeled and diced avocado, olives, tomatoes and cheese. Serve on a bed of lettuce.

cheese and fruit salad

1 cup cream or cottage
    cheese
1/3 cup chopped walnuts
2 rings canned or fresh
    pineapple, chopped

1 head iceberg or
    Romaine lettuce
1 large grapefruit
2 bananas
Juice of 1/2 lemon
French dressing

Combine cheese with nuts and pineapple.

Arrange lettuce on a platter, reserving some of the heart for garnish. Pile cheese in center.

Arrange segments of grapefruit and slices of banana brushed with lemon juice around cheese; tuck pieces of lettuce heart in between.

Pour dressing over top. If canned pineapple is used, 1 tablespoon pineapple juice can be substituted for 1 tablespoon oil in French dressing. Serves 4.

egg and kidney bean salad

4 hard-cooked eggs,
    chopped
16-ounce can kidney
    beans, well drained
1/2 cup sliced celery
1/4 cup chopped parsley
2 tablespoons finely
    chopped onion

3 tablespoons French
    dressing
1 teaspoon prepared
    mustard
1 teaspoon prepared
    horseradish
1/2 teaspoon salt
1/8 teaspoon pepper
Lettuce

Combine eggs, beans, celery, parsley, and onion.

Blend French dressing with seasonings; stir into egg mixture.

Chill at least 1 hour. Serve on crisp lettuce.
Serves 6.

creamy fruit salad

1 package (3 ounces)
    cream cheese
1 tablespoon syrup from
    canned mandarin
    oranges
1 can (11 ounces) man-
    darin orange sections,
    drained

1 can (13 1/2 ounces)
    pineapple tidbits,
    drained
1 cup miniature marsh-
    mallows
1/3 cup halved, drained
    maraschino cherries
Lettuce

Beat cream cheese with liquid from mandarin oranges until creamy.

Add oranges, pineapple, and marshmallows; combine gently but thoroughly. Lightly fold in cherries. Chill. Serve in lettuce cups.
Serves 6.

variation

Frozen fruit salad. Blend 1/4 cup mayonnaise with cream cheese and liquid before adding fruits. Whip 1 envelope dessert topping mix as directed on package label.

Fold whipped topping and cherries into fruit mixture. Pour into a 1 1/2-quart mold; freeze overnight. Dip in warm water to unmold.

exotic fruit salad

salad
1 head Bibb lettuce
½ cup sliced radishes
½ medium cucumber, thinly sliced
2 small tomatoes, sliced
1 green pepper, cleaned, seeded, and cut into slivers
1 cup diced fresh pineapple
1 cup fresh strawberries, cut in half
½ cup drained mandarin oranges
½ ripe avocado
1 large peach
2 tablespoons lemon juice

salad dressing
½ cup finely minced onion
½ teaspoon prepared mustard
6 tablespoons lemon juice
Salt
White pepper
3 tablespoons vegetable oil
¼ cup chopped parsley
2 tablespoons chopped fresh dill
½ teaspoon crumbled dried tarragon

First prepare dressing. Combine onion, mustard, lemon juice, salt and white pepper to taste, oil, parsley, dill, and tarragon. Mix well. Let stand at least ½ hour to blend flavors.

Wash lettuce, dry, break into bite-size pieces; place in large salad bowl. Add radishes, cucumber, tomatoes, green pepper, pineapple, strawberries, and mandarin oranges.

Just before serving, peel avocado half and peach, cut in wedges; dip in lemon juice. Add to salad.

Mix dressing again; pour over salad. Toss and serve. Serves 6.

spiced apple salad

1 cup granulated sugar
1 cup cold water
1 cup red hots (red cinnamon candies)
6 tart medium apples
1 cup creamed cottage cheese, small curd
½ cup finely chopped English walnuts
12 large lettuce leaves

Combine sugar, water, and cinnamon candies in saucepan. Cook over low heat until candy dissolves.

Pare and core apples. Place in syrup; cover, cook very slowly until apples are tender but not broken. Turn apples several times during cooking so they will be even in color. Remove apples from syrup; drain, chill thoroughly.

Mix cottage cheese and walnuts. Fill apple centers with cheese and nut mixture.

To serve, arrange filled apples on lettuce beds. Serves 6.

frozen fruit salad

1 16-ounce can dark
   sweet pitted cherries
1 16-ounce can
   pineapple tidbits
1 8-ounce package
   cream cheese,
   softened
2 cups whipped topping
½ cup chopped nuts
Crisp salad greens

Drain fruits well.

Beat cream cheese into whipped topping.

Fold in fruits and nuts.

Pour mixture into an 8- by 8-inch pan. Cover and freeze.

To serve, let salad set in the refrigerator about 1 hour.

Cut and serve on crisp salad greens. Serves 12.

crab-dressed salad

dressing
⅓ cup chili sauce
1 tablespoon finely cut
   scallions
2 teaspoons tarragon
   vinegar
2 teaspoons lemon juice
½ teaspoon salt
1½ cups plain yogurt
1 can (7½-ounce) king
   crab meat, drained
   and flaked

salad
1 bag (10-ounce) fresh
   spinach, washed,
   broken into bite-size
   pieces, chilled
6 ounces
   mozzarella cheese, cut
   into strips
1 stalk celery, sliced
¼ cup chopped parsley
Cucumber slices
Tomato wedges
Ripe olives

Combine chili sauce, scallions, vinegar, lemon juice, and salt; fold
in yogurt and crab meat. Cover; chill several hours. Prepare salad
greens by tossing together spinach, cheese, celery, and parsley in a
salad bowl. Garnish with cucumber slices, tomato wedges, and ripe
olives.

Pass dressing separately to serve. Serves 4 to 6.

avocado and strawberry salad

avocado and strawberry salad

½ cup almonds
1 8-ounce package
   cream cheese,
   softened
¾ cup confectioners'
   sugar
2 ripe avocados
Lemon juice
1 pint fresh straw-
   berries, cleaned
⅓ cup fresh orange juice

Spread almonds on cookie sheet; toast lightly in 350° F oven about 10 minutes. Blend, grind or chop finely.

Combine cream cheese and ½ cup confectioners' sugar in small mixing bowl; beat until fluffy. Stir in almonds. Shape into cone in center of serving dish.

Peel avocados; cut in half, remove seeds. Coat avocados generously with lemon juice to prevent darkening. Place 2 halves on opposite sides of cream cheese cone.

Arrange strawberries between avocado halves over cone. Slice remaining avocado; place around edge of serving dish, garnishing with any remaining strawberries.

Combine remaining confectioners' sugar with orange juice and 1 tablespoon lemon juice for sauce. Dust strawberries with additional confectioners' sugar. Spoon small amount of orange sauce over each serving. Serves 4 to 6.

11

health salad

1 head Boston lettuce
1 small cucumber
2 small tomatoes
1 green pepper
½ avocado
5 radishes
1 peach

1 slice pineapple (from can)
4 ounces mandarin oranges (from can)
¼ pound fresh strawberries

health salad

dressing
1 small onion, minced
2 teaspoons prepared mustard
6 tablespoons lemon juice
¼ teaspoon salt
⅛ teaspoon white pepper

3 tablespoons vegetable oil
1 sprig parsely, chopped
2 teaspoons fresh dill (or ½ teaspoon dried dill)
¼ teaspoon dried tarragon
¼ teaspoon dried basil

Wash lettuce; tear leaves in bite-size pieces. Cut unpeeled cucumber in thin slices. Peel tomatoes; cut in slices. Core, seed, and slice green pepper. Peel avocado; slice. Clean radishes; slice. Peel peach; cube peach and pineapple slice. Drain oranges. Hull and cut strawberries in half. Arrange all ingredients in a large bowl.

To make dressing, blend onion thoroughly with mustard, lemon juice, salt, pepper, and vegetable oil. Add herbs; correct seasoning if necessary. Pour over salad; mix gently but thoroughly. Cover salad; marinate about 10 minutes. Serve in a bowl or on a platter. Serves 4 to 6.

¾ pound cooked ham, cut in thick slices diced
¾ pound Gruyère cheese, diced
6 tablespoons olive oil
2 tablespoons white wine vinegar
Salt
Freshly ground black pepper
Romaine lettuce or curly endive
Finely chopped parsley or fresh herbs

swiss ham salad

Combine ham and cheese in a bowl.

Make dressing with oil, vinegar, salt and pepper. Pour over ham and cheese; toss lightly. Refrigerate; leave about 1 hour to marinate.

Arrange lettuce in a salad bowl. Pile ham and cheese in the center; sprinkle with parsley or herbs. Serves 4 to 5.

greek goddess salad

1 eggplant
Lemon juice
1 teaspoon salt
1 teaspoon oregano
¼ teaspoon garlic salt
½ cup olive oil
2 cups cooked, diced
   lamb
1 cup minced parsley
1 cup chopped celery

¼ cup sliced green
   onion
2 tomatoes, sliced
1 tablespoon sugar
1 tablespoon lemon
   juice
2 tablespoons vinegar
1 teaspoon mint
⅛ teaspoon pepper

Cut eggplant in half lengthwise. Scoop out pulp; dice.

Brush inside of eggplant shells with lemon juice. Cook; stir diced eggplant, salt, oregano and garlic salt in hot oil until tender. Remove to large bowl. Add lamb, parsley, celery, green onion, and tomatoes. Mix sugar, 1 tablespoon lemon juice, vinegar, mint and pepper. Pour over all, cover; chill 2 hours.

Fill eggplant shells to serve. Serves 2 to 4.

beef salad niçoise

8 slices rare cold roast
   beef
1 small cucumber
Salt
8 ripe tomatoes
2 green peppers
2 small chopped onions
   or 24 spring onions

3 lettuce hearts
3 hard-boiled eggs
   (optional)
16 anchovy filets
12 green olives
12 black olives

dressing
4 tablespoons best wine
   vinegar or lemon juice
12 tablespoons best
   olive oil

1 large teaspoon French
   mustard
¼ teaspoon sugar
2 cloves crushed garlic

Prepare ingredients for salad. Cut slices of beef into thin strips. Slice cucumber, salt; allow to stand 10 minutes; wash and drain in cold water. Quarter and seed tomatoes; seed and slice peppers; wash and chop onions or top spring onions. Break up and wash lettuce; discard outer leaves. Hard-boil eggs. Soak anchovies in milk 10 minutes to remove salt; drain. Pit olives.

Arrange lettuce leaves round large salad bowl or dish. Put ingredients into bowl in layers, reserving anchovies and olives for top. Arrange top layer carefully with an eye to color. Make lattice design over whole top with anchovies, putting an olive in center of each lattice alternating the colors.

Mix all ingredients for dressing together; spoon over whole salad. Serve cold with garlic bread or French bread and butter. Serves 8.

luncheon salad

2 cups chopped cooked
   meat or poultry
2 cups grated raw carrot
2 tablespoons finely
   chopped onion
2 unpeeled dessert
   apples, cored and
   chopped
3 to 4 stalks celery,
   chopped

2 teaspoons French
   mustard
½ cup mayonnaise
Salt
Lettuce
1 tablespoon chopped
   parsley
Cranberry or apple jelly

Combine meat, carrot, onion, apple and celery in a bowl.

Mix mustard with mayonnaise, add to ingredients in bowl; toss lightly together. Add a little salt to taste.

Arrange "cups" of lettuce on individual dishes. Pile mixture in center, sprinkle with parsley; top with a spoonful of jelly. Serves 4 to 5.

note

Any kind of cooked meat or poultry can be used in this salad.

egg and veal salad

6 hard-cooked eggs,
   chopped
2 cups cooked veal,
   diced
1 cup green beans,
   cooked or canned, cut
   in ½-inch pieces
½ cup celery, sliced
½ cup sweet or dill
   pickle, chopped

2 tablespoons pickle
   liquid
½ teaspoon salt
¼ teaspoon pepper
⅓ cup salad dressing
Salad greens
1 or 2 tomatoes, cut in
   wedges

Combine eggs, veal, beans, celery, and pickle.

Blend pickle liquid, salt, and pepper with salad dressing. Stir into egg mixture. Chill.

Serve on crisp salad greens; garnish with tomato wedges. Serves 6.

bavarian sausage salad

½ pound knockwurst,
   cooked and cooled
2 small pickles
1 onion
3 tablespoons vinegar
1 teaspoon strong
   mustard
2 tablespoons vegetable
   oil

½ teaspoon salt
¼ teaspoon pepper
¼ teaspoon paprika
¼ teaspoon sugar
1 tablespoon capers
1 tablespoon chopped
   parsley

Cut knockwurst into small cubes. Mince pickles and onion.

Mix together vinegar, mustard, and oil. Add salt, pepper, paprika, and sugar. Adjust seasonings if desired. Add capers; mix well. Stir in chopped knockwurst, pickles, and onions.

Just before serving, garnish with chopped parsley. Serves 4.

fruit-meat salad

½ medium-size head
   lettuce
1 medium-size grapefruit
1 medium-size orange
1 cup cut-up canned
   luncheon meat

1 stalk celery
Salt and pepper to taste
Sugar to taste
2 tablespoons Italian
   salad dressing

Tear or cut lettuce into bite-size pieces. Put in large bowl.

Peel and section grapefruit and orange. Put in bowl. Add meat.
Cut up celery; add to salad.

Sprinkle with salt, pepper, and sugar. Add salad dressing. Toss to
mix. Serves 4.

variation
Fruit-cheese salad. Use 1 cup cut-up cheese in place of meat.

liverwurst salad

1 cup diced liverwurst
¼ cup finely chopped
   onion
¼ cup diced celery
¼ cup finely chopped
   green pepper
½ head lettuce, torn into
   medium-size pieces
½ cup shredded carrots

salad dressing
⅓ cup salad oil
⅓ cup salad vinegar
⅓ cup chili sauce
1 tablespoon prepared
   horseradish
½ teaspoon salt

Combine liverwurst, onion, celery, green pepper, lettuce, and carrots in salad bowl. Chill mixture thoroughly.

Combine dressing ingredients in a jar; shake vigorously. Chill.

To serve, place vegetable and meat mixture in salad bowls. Pour
dressing mixture into a small pitcher and pass to guests. Serves 6.

molded pineapple-carrot salad

1 package (3 ounces)
   lemon-flavored gelatin
1 cup shredded raw
   carrots
1 can (10½ ounces)
   crushed pineapple,
   drained
¼ cup raisins
Lettuce
Mayonnaise

Prepare gelatin according to package directions, using pineapple
syrup as part of the liquid. Chill until mixture is slightly thickened.

Fold in carrots, pineapple, and raisins; pour into a 1-quart mold.
Chill until firm. Serve on lettuce; top with mayonnaise if desired.
Serves 6.

jellied vegetable salad

1 3-ounce package
   lemon flavored gelatin
1 teaspoon unflavored
   gelatin
1 cup boiling water
1 cup cold water
1 teaspoon finely
   chopped onion
½ teaspoon salt
¼ cup chopped green
   pepper
¼ cup shredded carrots
¼ cup diced celery
¼ cup thinly sliced
   radishes
Lettuce

Combine flavored and unflavored gelatin. Dissolve in boiling water. Add cold water, onion, and salt. Chill in refrigerator until mixture begins to thicken.

Gently stir in green pepper, carrots, celery, and radishes. Pour into a 1-quart mold or six individual molds. Chill until set. Unmold by dipping mold in pan of warm water a few seconds.

Serve on lettuce. Serves 6.

jellied tomato ring

4 cups tomato juice
2 teaspoons salt
¼ teaspoon freshly
   ground black pepper
¼ teaspoon finely
   chopped basil
1 onion, peeled and
   finely chopped
2 envelopes gelatin
¼ cup cold water
2 teaspoons prepared
   horseradish
2 tablespoons sugar
2 tablespoons lemon
   juice
¼ pound elbow
   macaroni, cooked
Lettuce

Put tomato juice, seasoning, basil and onion into a skillet. Heat to boiling point; simmer 10 minutes. Strain.

Soak gelatin in cold water 5 minutes. Add to hot tomato juice; stir until dissolved. Add horseradish, sugar and lemon juice, adjust seasoning to taste. Set aside to chill until mixture begins to thicken.

Stir in cooked macaroni; pour into a lightly-oiled 9-inch ring mold. Chill until set.

Unmold onto shredded lettuce; fill center as desired. Serves 4 to 6.

note
The center can be filled with any meat, poultry or fish mixture.

caribbean salad

caribbean salad

2 tablespoons vinegar
½ teaspoon salt
⅛ teaspoon white
   pepper
1 teaspoon honey
3 drops angostura
   bitters
½ small onion, grated
2 tablespoons vegetable
   oil

2 medium bananas
2 medium tomatoes
2 mandarin oranges (or
   1 small can, drained)
1 4½-ounce can shrimps
Parsley for garnish
4 stuffed olives for
   garnish

Make salad dressing by combining and blending vinegar, salt, pepper, honey, bitters, onion, and oil. Adjust seasonings to taste.

Peel and slice bananas and add immediately to dressing to prevent browning. Peel tomatoes and cut into quarters; peel oranges and section (remove all white membrane). Add tomatoes and oranges to dressing. Carefully stir in drained shrimps.

Arrange salad in an attractive bowl and garnish with parsley and stuffed halved olives. Serves 4.

cottage cheese-fruit mold

1 3-ounce package lime
   or orange gelatin
1 cup boiling water
1 cup pineapple liquid
   and water
1 8-ounce can crushed
   pineapple, drained

1 pound cottage cheese,
   uncreamed
1 cup seedless grapes,
   halved
1 tablespoon lemon
   juice, if desired
Lettuce

Dissolve gelatin in boiling water. Add pineapple liquid. Chill until thick but not set.

Stir in remaining ingredients except lettuce. Pour into 8-inch square pan. Chill overnight or until set.

Serve on lettuce. Serves 6.

19

1 cup macaroni
4 cups salted water
2 cups diced cooked
  ham
1 banana
2 tablespoons lemon
  juice

1 stalk celery
½ small honeydew
  melon
1 small bunch Concord
  grapes
1 cup small peas

ham salad

marinade
½ cup sour cream
2 tablespoons
  mayonnaise

1 tablespoon lemon
  juice
Salt and pepper to taste
Pinch of sugar

Place macaroni in boiling water 12 to 15 minutes. Drain macaroni, cool with cold water; let it stand to dry. Mix cold macaroni and diced ham in large bowl.

Peel and slice banana; let stand with half of lemon juice. Chop celery; mix with rest of lemon juice.

Remove seeds from melon; cut into bite-size pieces. Seed and halve grapes. Drain liquid from peas. Mix all fruit and peas with banana and celery; combine with macaroni and ham.

Mix sour cream and mayonnaise well. Add the rest of ingredients. Spread marinade over salad; cover.

Refrigerate salad at least 60 minutes before serving. Serves 6 to 8.

ham salad

marinated beef salad

salad
3 cups cubed cooked lean beef
½ cup chopped onion
2 tablespoons chopped parsley

salad dressing
½ cup olive oil
¼ cup wine vinegar
½ teaspoon salt
¼ teaspoon pepper

garnish
1 head Boston lettuce
1 large tomato, cut in wedges

1 sweet red pepper, seeded and chopped
1 medium tomato, chopped

½ teaspoon crumbled oregano
½ teaspoon prepared mustard

Combine beef, onion, parsley, red pepper, and tomato, tossing well.

Combine olive oil, vinegar, salt, pepper, oregano, and mustard; pour over salad, tossing well. Refrigerate at least 3 hours.

At serving time line serving dish with lettuce leaves, fill with salad; garnish with tomato wedges. Serve with plenty of crusty bread. Serves 4.

marinated beef salad

creamy golden waldorf

creamy golden waldorf

1 6-ounce package lemon gelatin
¼ teaspoon salt
⅔ cup hot water
Lemon juice
3 medium golden delicious apples
½ cup mayonnaise

1 cup heavy cream, whipped
1 cup finely chopped celery
1 cup finely chopped walnuts
Salad greens

Dissolve gelatin and salt in hot water in a bowl; stir in 2 tablespoons lemon juice. Chill until thickened.

Pare 2 apples partially; core and dice. Skin will add color to salad. Core and cut remaining apple into thin slices. Sprinkle diced and sliced apples with lemon juice to prevent discoloration. Arrange apple slices, skin side down, around bottom of an 8-cup mold.

Blend mayonnaise into thickened gelatin; fold in whipped cream. Fold in diced apples, celery and walnuts gently; spoon carefully over apple slices. Chill until firm.

Unmold onto salad platter; garnish with salad greens. Serves 6 to 8.

bleu cheese-spinach mold

2 envelopes unflavored gelatin
½ cup cold water
1 can (13¼ ounces) beef broth, heated to boiling
½ cup bottled chunky bleu cheese dressing
1 small onion, quartered
¼ teaspoon salt
2 tablespoons lemon juice
1 package (10 ounces) frozen chopped spinach, thawed and drained
1 cup finely chopped cucumber, seeded, pared
½ cup chopped celery

In electric blender, sprinkle gelatin over cold water. In small saucepan heat beef broth to boiling; add to gelatin. Cover, process at low speed until gelatin dissolves.

Add bleu cheese dressing and onion; cover, process until smooth. Add salt, lemon juice, and spinach; cover, process just until smooth.

Turn into bowl; chill, stirring occasionally, until mixture mounds slightly when dropped from a spoon. Fold in cucumber and celery. Turn into 4-cup mold. Chill until set.

To serve, unmold; garnish with tomatoes and parsley or tiny spinach leaves. Serves 8.

super salmon mousse

1 cup mayonnaise
3 stalks celery, cut-up
1 medium onion, cut-up
8 ounces cream cheese, room temperature
2 envelopes unflavored gelatin
1 can undiluted tomato soup
½ teaspoon seafood seasoning
4 to 5 drops liquid smoke
1 large can red salmon (15½ ounces)
1 small can red salmon (7 ounces)

Place mayonnaise, celery, onion and cream cheese in blender. Puree until smooth. Dissolve gelatin in hot soup. Add soup and seasonings to blender; mix until smooth.

Carefully flake salmon after it has been well drained. Mash with fork or fingers until fine.

In large mixing bowl, combine blender ingredients and salmon. Thoroughly mix together by hand. Pour mixture into a large greased fish-shaped mold; refrigerate overnight until set. After about 1 hour in the refrigerator, cover mousse carefully with plastic wrap.

Serve with sliced black or rye cocktail bread. Do not freeze.

variation
Tuna may be substituted for salmon, if desired.

chicken salad

¼ pound mushrooms
½ cup French dressing
1 large iceberg lettuce
1½ cups diced cooked
  chicken
1 can artichoke hearts,
  drained and cut into
  strips

1 small red pepper,
  seeded and cut into
  strips
½ pound cooked green
  beans, sliced
1 cup grapes, halved and
  seeded
¼ cup toasted flaked
  almonds

Wash and slice mushrooms; place in a shallow bowl. Pour French dressing over; set aside 1 hour, stirring occasionally.

Wash lettuce, discarding outer leaves; line a deep salad bowl or large platter.

Combine chicken, artichoke hearts, red pepper and beans. Add mushrooms and dressing, season to taste; toss all lightly together. Refrigerate until ready to serve; spoon chicken mixture over lettuce.

Sprinkle with grapes and toasted almonds. Serves 5 to 6.

chicken-apple salad

2 cups cooked chicken,
  diced
2 cups diced apples,
  unpared
½ cup chopped celery
½ cup raisins

1 tablespoon lemon
  juice
½ cup salad dressing,
  mayonnaise type
6 lettuce cups

Mix all ingredients except lettuce. Chill thoroughly.

Serve in lettuce cups. Serves 6.

variations

cheese-apple salad. Omit chicken, raisins, and lemon juice. Use 3 cups diced apples and 1 cup grated cheddar cheese.

ham-apple salad. In place of chicken, use 2 cups cooked, diced ham.

tuna-apple salad. In place of chicken, use two 6½- or 7-ounce cans tuna, drained and broken into large pieces.

turkey-apple salad. In place of chicken, use 2 cups cooked, diced turkey.

turkey kidney bean salad

1 cup leftover turkey
  pieces
1¼ cups cooked or
  canned, drained
  kidney beans
⅓ cup chopped sweet
  pickle
⅔ cup coarsely chopped
  celery
1 tablespoon finely
  chopped onion

2 diced hard-cooked
  eggs
1 teaspoon salt
3 tablespoons
  mayonnaise
1 teaspoon pickle liquid
1 teaspoon prepared
  mustard

Combine all ingredients. Toss lightly. Chill at least one hour to blend flavors. Serves 6.

mexicana chicken-rice salad

2 tablespoons salad oil
2 tablespoons vinegar
1 teaspoon prepared
 mustard
½ teaspoon salt
⅛ teaspoon chili
 powder
2 cups brown rice,
 cooked
2 cups cooked chicken,
 chopped

1 cup thinly sliced celery
½ cup thinly sliced green
 pepper
¼ cup chopped dill
 pickle
2 tablespoons finely
 chopped onion
½ cup mayonnaise
2 hard-cooked eggs,
 chopped

Mix salad oil, vinegar, mustard, salt, chili powder, and rice.

Chill several hours or overnight.

Add remaining ingredients; mix gently. Chill until served. Serves 6.

variation
Mexicana turkey-rice salad. Use turkey instead of chicken.

chicken salad with litchis

3 cups cooked diced
 chicken
2-3 stalks celery,
 chopped
1 green pepper, chopped
Salt
Pepper
¾ cup French dressing
Salad greens
1 can litchis
1 small can mandarins

dressing
¾ cup mayonnaise
¼ cup sour cream
2 teaspoons curry
 powder
2 tablespoons grated
 onion
2 tablespoons chopped
 parsley

Combine chicken, celery and green pepper. Add salt, pepper and French dressing. Toss lightly together; chill about ½ hour.

Arrange some salad greens round a large platter; pile chicken mixture in center.

Drain litchis and mandarins. Place a mandarin segment in each litchi; and arrange round the edge or down the center.

Blend all ingredients for dressing together, chill well; serve dressing separately. Serves 5 to 6.

chicken salad with asparagus

1 3-pound chicken
½ teaspoon salt
⅛ teaspoon pepper
¼ teaspoon paprika
1 16-ounce can peas, drained
1 14½-ounce can asparagus pieces, drained
1 8-ounce can sliced mushrooms, drained
1 8-ounce container plain yogurt
2 tablespoons mayonnaise
1 teaspoon dillweed
½ teaspoon salt
⅛ teaspoon pepper

Place chicken in center of a large square of aluminum foil. Sprinkle with salt, pepper, and paprika. Wrap. Cook in preheated 350°F oven 1 hour. Cool. Remove meat from bone. Cut into bite-size pieces.

In a large bowl, add chicken, peas, asparagus, and mushrooms. Mix together yogurt, mayonnaise, dillweed, salt, and pepper; gently combine with other ingredients. Marinate in refrigerator 2 hours before serving. Serves 6.

chicken salad supreme

2 whole broiler-fryer chicken breasts
2 broiler-fryer chicken thighs
2 broiler-fryer chicken drumsticks
2½ cups water
2 teaspoons salt, divided
½ teaspoon pepper, divided
3 celery tops
1 small onion, sliced
½ bunch green onions, minced
1 cup finely chopped celery
½ cup chopped English walnuts
¼ cup finely chopped fresh parsley
1 tablespoon orange juice
¾ cup plus 2 tablespoons mayonnaise, divided
½ pound romaine lettuce, shredded
2 hard-cooked eggs, sieved
1 jar (4 ounces) pimento

In deep saucepan place chicken. Add water, 1 teaspoon salt, ¼ teaspoon pepper, celery tops and sliced onion. Cover and simmer about 45 minutes or until fork can be inserted in chicken with ease.

Remove chicken from broth. Cool. Remove skin. From one whole chicken breast cut meat in slices; set aside. Separate meat from bones of remaining pieces.

Cut chicken in bite-size pieces; place in large mixing bowl. Add green onion, chopped celery, remaining 1 teaspoon salt, remaining ¼ teaspoon pepper, nuts and parsley. In bowl mix orange juice with ¾ cup mayonnaise; stir into chicken mixture.

On serving platter arrange lettuce. Spoon chicken mixture on lettuce. In bowl mix eggs and remaining 2 tablespoons mayonnaise. Spread egg mixture over chicken mixture. Place chicken slices on top, evenly spaced. Place pimento between slices. Serves 4.

fruit and crab salad

1 6-ounce package
  lemon gelatin
2 cups cold water
½ teaspoon crushed
  rosemary
1 cup fresh orange
  sections
1 cup fresh grapefruit
  sections
1 pound fresh crab meat
  or 2 6-ounce packages
  frozen Alaskan king
  crab, thawed

½ cup chopped onion
1 tablespoon chopped
  fresh parsley
3 drops of hot sauce
⅓ cup mayonnaise
1 teaspoon prepared
  mustard
¾ cup sliced celery

Dissolve gelatin in 2 cups boiling water. Add 2 cups cold water; chill until partially set. Fold in rosemary, orange and grapefruit sections; spoon into 1½-quart ring mold. Chill until firm.

Drain crab, cut into large pieces; place in a medium-sized bowl. Mix onion with parsley, hot sauce, mayonnaise, mustard and celery. Pour over crab; and toss until mixed. Chill.

Unmold gelatin mixture onto large serving plate; fill center with the crab mixture. Garnish with salad greens; serve immediately. Serves 6.

fruit and crab salad

3 cups diced cooked chicken
1 cup chopped celery
¼ cup chopped red sweet pepper (optional)
½ teaspoon salt
½ teaspoon pepper
⅔ cup bleu cheese dressing

2 cups orange sections
2 cups grapefruit sections
½ cup diced avocado
1 avocado, cut in wedges
Orange or grapefruit juice
Salad greens

sorrento salad

Combine chicken, celery, and red pepper in a bowl; sprinkle with salt and pepper. Add bleu cheese dressing; toss to mix well. Chill thoroughly.

Dice enough orange and grapefruit sections to make ½ cup of each. Add to chicken mixture. Coat diced avocado and avocado wedges with orange juice. Add diced avocado to the chicken mixture.

Line large salad bowl with salad greens; spoon salad into bowl. Arrange remaining orange and grapefruit sections and avocado wedges around salad.

Serve with additional bleu cheese dressing. Serves 6.

sorrento salad

3 cups cooked turkey or chicken, diced
1 cup diced celery
½ teaspoon salt
⅛ teaspoon pepper
1 tablespoon minced onion

1 tablespoon lemon juice, if desired
½ cup mayonnaise or salad dressing or
⅓ cup French dressing

turkey or chicken salad

Mix all ingredients gently. Chill before serving. Serves 6.

variation
turkey- or chicken-fruit salad. Omit 1 cup of the turkey or chicken. Add 1 cup seedless grapes or pineapple chunks.

2 cans (6½ or 7 ounces each) tuna
or
1 can (1 pound) salmon
1 cup chopped celery
⅓ cup mayonnaise or salad dressing

2 hard-cooked eggs, chopped
2 tablespoons chopped onion
2 tablespoons chopped sweet pickle
Salad greens

simple seafood salad

Drain fish. Break fish into large pieces. Combine all ingredients except salad greens. Toss lightly. Chill.

Serve on salad greens. Serves 6.

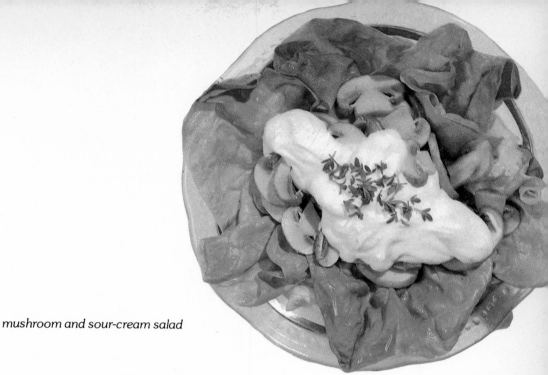

mushroom and sour-cream salad

artichoke and tomato salad

**2 4-ounce jars marinated
    artichoke hearts**
½ cup sauterne
Juice of lemon
1 whole fennel
**6 medium tomatoes,
    sliced**

2 small onions, diced
1 clove garlic
½ teaspoon salt
**¼ teaspoon white
    pepper**
½ cup warm beef broth

Drain artichoke hearts, reserving marinade. Cut the artichoke hearts in half; place in large salad bowl. Combine reserved marinade, wine, and lemon juice; pour over artichoke hearts.

Clean fennel, wash and slice. Add to artichoke hearts. Add tomatoes and onions.

Mash garlic clove with the salt and pepper; add to beef broth. Mix well; pour over vegetables. Marinate at least 10 minutes.

Serve with crusty bread. Serves 6 to 8.

note
If fennel is unavailable, substitute 1 small bunch of celery, cleaned and sliced.

artichoke and tomato salad

herring salad with sour cream

sour-cream sauce
1 cup sour cream
½ cup yogurt
Juice of ½ lemon
¼ teaspoon sugar

salad
2 small onions
2 tart apples
8 marinated herring
   fillets
2 teaspoons fresh dill or
   ½ teaspoon dried
   dillweed

herring salad with sour cream

To prepare sauce, blend thoroughly sour cream, yogurt, lemon juice, and sugar.

Peel onions; cut into thin slices. Peel and quarter apples, remove cores; cut into thin wedges. Blend onions and apples with sauce.

In a dish arrange herring and apple-onion mixture in layers. Cover tightly; marinate in refrigerator 5 hours.

Sprinkle with dill before serving. Serves 4 to 6.

marinated tomatoes

4 large tomatoes, peeled and sliced
1 cup vegetable oil
¼ cup wine vinegar
¼ teaspoon dry mustard
1 teaspoon salt
¼ teaspoon black pepper

1 large clove garlic, minced
1 tablespoon chopped fresh basil
2 sprigs fresh thyme, chopped
1 sprig fresh marjoram, chopped
1 tablespoon minced scallion

Place tomato slices in serving bowl. Combine remaining ingredients; pour over tomatoes. Toss lightly.

Chill 1 hour or longer before serving. Serves 4.

mixed-vegetable salad

2 cups finely shredded raw cabbage
2 cups finely shredded raw carrots
2 cups finely shredded raw beets
2 cups seeded, finely shredded raw cucumbers

1½ cups thinly sliced radishes
1½ cups tomatoes
1½ cups French dressing

Crisp cabbage, carrots, beets, cucumbers, and radishes in bowls of salt water. Skin, seed, and shred tomatoes.

Drain all vegetables and fruit when firm and crisp. Arrange in a deep salad bowl in circular heaps so that colors add to eye-appeal of salad.

Just before serving, pour French dressing over all. Serves 8.

mushroom and sour-cream salad

2 cups canned mushroom slices, drained
½ cup wine vinegar
4 heads Boston lettuce
½ cup sour cream
1 tablespoon chopped fresh parsley

Combine mushroom slices and vinegar; marinate in refrigerator 24 hours. Drain.

Arrange lettuce on salad plate. Place ½ cup marinated mushrooms in center of lettuce bed; garnish with 2 tablespoons sour cream and fresh parsley. Serves 4.

31

seafood salad with mayonnaise

3 cups cooked seafood (any one or a combination of crab, shrimp, or lobster)
½ cup chopped celery
½ cup sliced green onions
½ teaspoon dried dillweed

2 tablespoons olive oil
2 tablespoons lemon juice
4 medium tomatoes
2 hard-cooked eggs, sliced
Lemon wedges
Lettuce

caper mayonnaise
1 egg
½ teaspoon mustard
½ teaspoon salt
Dash cayenne pepper
½ teaspoon sugar

1 cup olive oil
3 tablespoons lemon juice
2 tablespoons capers, chopped

In a mixing bowl combine the seafood, celery, onions, dill, 2 tablespoons olive oil, and 2 tablespoons lemon juice. Mix well. Refrigerate until ready to use.

Slice the tops off the tomatoes. Scoop out the pulp and reserve for another purpose, leaving a shell approximately ½ inch thick. Drain.

Next, make the Caper Mayonnaise. In a blender container combine the egg, mustard, salt, pepper, sugar, and ¼ cup of the oil. Blend thoroughly. With the blender running, very slowly add ½ cup more oil. Then add the lemon juice gradually and the remaining ¼ cup of oil. Blend until thick, occasionally scraping the sides of the blender jar.

Transfer to a serving bowl and fold in the capers.

Arrange the lettuce on individual plates. Place one tomato shell on each plate and stuff with seafood mixture. Garnish with hard-cooked eggs and lemon wedges and serve with Caper Mayonnaise. Serves 4.

sardine and beet salad

8 sardines, chopped
2 large boiled beets, diced
1 medium onion, minced
4 tablespoons oil
4 tablespoons vinegar
1 teaspoon salt
Dash of cayenne pepper
Chopped parsley for garnish

Put together sardines, beets, and onion in a large bowl.

Mix oil, vinegar, salt, and pepper together until well-blended. Pour over sardine mixture.

Garnish with parsley on top. Serves 6.

chef's salad chesapeake

1 can (12 ounces) blue
  crab meat or other
  crab meat, fresh,
  frozen, or pasteurized
  or
2 cans (6½ or 7½
  ounces each) crab
  meat

1 package (10 ounces)
  frozen asparagus
  spears
6 lettuce cups
Lemon-Caper Dressing
3 hard-cooked eggs,
  sliced
Paprika

Thaw frozen crab meat. Drain. Remove any remaining shell or cartilage. Flake crab meat.

Cook asparagus spears according to directions on package. Drain; chill. Place 3 asparagus spears in each lettuce cup.

Place about ⅓ cup crab meat on asparagus. Cover with approximately 2 tablespoons Lemon-Caper Dressing. Top with 3 slices hard-cooked egg. Sprinkle with paprika. Serves 6.

lemon-caper dressing

½ cup low calorie salad
  dressing (mayonnaise
  type)
1 tablespoon drained
  capers
1 tablespoon lemon
  juice

½ teaspoon prepared
  mustard
½ teaspoon Worcester-
  shire sauce
2 drops liquid hot
  pepper sauce

Combine all ingredients. Chill. Makes approximately ⅔ cup salad dressing.

scallop-vegetable salad

1½ pounds scallops,
  fresh or frozen
1 quart boiling water
2 tablespoons salt
1 can (1 pound) cut
  green beans, drained
1 cup sliced celery

¼ cup chopped onion
¼ cup chopped green
  pepper
1 tablespoon chopped
  pimento
Marinade
6 lettuce cups

Thaw frozen scallops. Rinse with cold water to remove any shell particles. Place in boiling salted water. Cover; return to boiling point. Reduce heat; simmer 3 to 4 minutes, depending on size. Drain and cool. Slice scallops.

Combine all ingredients except lettuce. Cover; chill at least 1 hour. Drain. Serve in lettuce cups. Serves 6.

marinade

½ cup cider vinegar
1 tablespoon sugar
¼ teaspoon salt

Dash of pepper
¼ cup salad oil

Combine vinegar, sugar, salt, and pepper. Add oil gradually, blending thoroughly. Makes approximately ⅔ cup marinade.

turkey salad in curried mayonnaise

3 cups turkey meat
3 cups mixed cooked
    vegetables, peas,
    beans, corn, celery
    and pimento
4 tomatoes
1 bunch watercress
1 teaspoon butter
1 shallot (or 1 table-
    spoon chopped onion)
½ tablespoon curry
    powder

1 teaspoon flour
½ cup stock
2 teaspoons coconut
2 teaspoons chutney
3 teaspoons lemon juice
Salt
Pepper
1 - 1½ cups mayonnaise
A pinch of paprika
1 - 2 lemons

Cook vegetables separately; let cool. Shred cold turkey. Quarter tomatoes, remove seeds; strain, reserve juice for thinning mayonnaise. Wash watercress; dry thoroughly.

Make curry flavoring. Melt butter, cook chopped shallot or onion until tender. Add curry powder or paste; cook a minute or two. Sprinkle in flour; cook 1 minute. Add stock; blend well. Bring to boil, stirring all the time. Sprinkle on coconut, add chutney and lemon juice; cook 10 to 15 minutes. Strain; let cool. Add lemon juice, salt and pepper. When cold, add to mayonnaise.

To mayonnaise add cooled curry mixture to taste. Add as much of strained tomato juice as will make spooning consistency.

Mix all vegetables together; season with salt and pepper, sprinkle with lemon juice. Put into dish or salad bowl. Arrange turkey shreds in center; spoon mayonnaise carefully over top, allowing vegetable salad to show around edges. Sprinkle top with paprika. Arrange tomato quarters and small sprigs of watercress alternately around edge of dish; serve with lemon quarters separately. Serves 4 to 6.

gulf shrimp salad

3 cans (4½ or 5 ounces
    each) shrimp
2 cups cooked rice
1 cup sliced celery
½ cup chopped parsley
¼ cup sliced ripe olives
½ cup mayonnaise or
    salad dressing

2 tablespoons French
    dressing
2 tablespoons lemon
    juice
1 teaspoon curry powder
Salad greens

Drain shrimp. Cover with ice water; stand 5 minutes. Drain. Cut large shrimp in half. Combine rice, celery, parsley, olives, and shrimp.

Combine mayonnaise, French dressing, lemon juice, and curry powder; mix thoroughly. Add mayonnaise mixture to shrimp mixture; toss lightly. Chill.

Serve on salad greens. Serves 6.

VEGETABLES

fried artichokes

8 small artichokes
Juice of 1 lemon
4 tablespoons flour
Bowl of cold water
2 eggs

1 tablespoon warm
water
Fat for deep-frying
¾ cup bread crumbs

Peel tough outer leaves from artichokes. Slice 1 inch off tips and small portion of stem. Cut artichokes in half lengthwise; remove the purple choke. Scrape upper portion and stem to remove any dark green.

Add lemon juice and flour to bowl of cold water. Drop artichoke hearts into bowl as you work. Drain just before cooking.

Parboil artichoke hearts in boiling salted water 30 to 45 minutes or until tender. Drain well.

Dip artichoke hearts in eggs and then in bread crumbs; dip in again. Fry in hot fat (365°F) until brown.

Drain on paper towels and serve. Serves 4.

variations
Any of the following vegetables can be breaded and fried in the above manner.

Eggplant (1 pound): Cut into slices ½ inch thick. Soak in salted water before breading. Drain, dip in egg and water mixture and then in crumbs. Dip again. Shallow-fry in hot oil until golden.

Squash (1 pound): Cut into slices ½ inch thick. Do not parboil. Bread and deep-fry, using same method as for artichoke hearts.

Cauliflower (1 medium head): Clean cauliflower head, separate into florets, and parboil in salted water until crisp-tender. Drain well. Bread and deep-fry, using same method as for artichoke hearts.

fresh asparagus

**Asparagus, as many as
  are needed, allowing
  4 to 6 per person**
½ cup boiling water
½ teaspoon salt
Melted butter
Lemon juice

Cut away fibrous part of asparagus stalks. Tie together, place in a tall pot.

Add boiling water and salt. Cover; cook over medium heat about 8 minutes. Do not overcook. Drain.

Pour over asparagus melted butter to which a little lemon juice has been added.

1 tablespoon margarine
**2 medium onions, sliced
  in rings**
**2 cups bean sprouts (1
  1-pound can, drained)**
½ teaspoon salt
**1 teaspoon soy sauce
  (optional)**
1 teaspoon lemon juice

Melt margarine in medium skillet; lightly tan onions. Add rest of ingredients, stirring to blend flavors. Cover skillet; simmer 1 minute. Serve at once. Serves 4 to 6.

36

baked beans with molasses

½ pound salt pork
3 cans (1 pound size)
  baked beans
1 tablespoon dry
  mustard
2 tablespoons molasses

2 tablespoons cognac
  (optional)
1 teaspoon salt
Dash of pepper
1 small onion
Grated rind of ½ lemon

Preheat oven to 325°F. Slice salt pork; cook in boiling water 10 minutes. Drain.

Put beans in bean pot or 2-quart casserole. Mix mustard, molasses, cognac, salt, pepper, grated onion, and lemon rind; pour over beans, lay salt pork on top. Bake, uncovered, 1½ to 2 hours. Add a little boiling water during baking if beans look dry. Serves 6.

asparagus pie

pastry
2 cups all purpose flour
½ teaspoon salt
½ cup shortening
3 to 4 tablespoons milk

filling
2 cans (about 8 ounces
  each) asparagus
  spears
2 tablespoons butter or
  margarine
3 tablespoons flour
1 cup milk
A pinch of cayenne
  pepper
1 cup grated cheese
3 to 4 tablespoons heavy
  cream
2 eggs

Pre-heat oven to 400°F.

Make pastry in usual way but use milk instead of water for mixing. Chill as long as possible; roll out, line a 9-inch pie plate.

Drain asparagus; arrange spears in a wheel shape in pastry shell. Set aside in a cool place while making sauce.

Melt butter in pan, stir in flour; cook 2 minutes stirring constantly. Add milk gradually; stir until boiling. Add seasoning, grated cheese, cream and beaten egg yolks. Fold in stiffly-beaten egg whites.

Pour over asparagus, bake 30 to 40 minutes; serve with broiled tomatoes and green salad. Serves 5 to 6.

lima beans and peppers

lima beans and peppers

1 10-ounce package
  frozen baby lima
  beans
3 tablespoons olive oil
½ cup green pepper, cut
  into thin strips

¼ cup sweet red pepper,
  cut into thin strips
¼ cup finely chopped
  onion

Cook beans in boiling salted water, according to package directions. Drain; keep warm.

Heat oil in small skillet. Add green pepper, red pepper, and onion; sauté 5 minutes.

Combine lima bean and pepper mixture gently. Serve immediately. Serves 4.

green beans plaki

1½ pounds green beans
¼ cup olive oil
2 medium onions,
  chopped
Juice of 1 lemon
¾ teaspoon salt

¼ teaspoon pepper
⅓ cup bread crumbs
¾ teaspoon dried savory
1 bunch parsley,
  chopped
2 cups hot water

Clean beans, wash, and cut in half.

Heat oil in large saucepan. Layer beans, onions, lemon juice, salt, pepper, bread crumbs, and herbs, reserving ½ cup parsley for garnish. Last layer should be beans. Add water. Cook over low heat 30 to 35 minutes or until beans are tender. Garnish with parsley; cool.

Serve cold as an accompaniment to a main dish. Serves 6.

38

refried beans

1½ cups dry kidney
   beans
5 cups water or stock
1 cup chopped onion
2 medium tomatoes,
   chopped

½ teaspoon garlic
1 teaspoon chili powder
Cayenne pepper
1 teaspoon salt
Oil

Soak beans overnight; cook with ½ cup onions, tomatoes, ¼ teaspoon garlic, chili, cayenne and water. When tender, add salt.

In large frying pan heat oil; sauté remaining onion and garlic until onion is transparent. Add tomato mixture. Mash ¼ cup beans into mixture; continue mashing and adding beans by quarter cups. Cook about 10 minutes longer. Serves 4 to 6.

harvard beets

12 small beets
½ cup sugar
1½ teaspoons
   cornstarch
¼ cup vinegar
¼ cup water
2 tablespoons butter

Cook and dice beets. Mix sugar, cornstarch, vinegar and water in a pan; boil 5 minutes. Add beets, let stand 30 minutes. Just before serving, bring to boiling point; add 2 tablespoons butter. Serves 6.

paprika-buttered broccoli

1 cup water
1 teaspoon salt
2 10-ounce packages
   frozen whole broccoli

paprika butter
¼ cup butter
½ teaspoon salt
¼ teaspoon white
   pepper
¼ teaspoon paprika

Bring water to rapid boil in saucepan. Add 1 teaspoon salt and broccoli; continue to boil for 15 minutes or until broccoli is fork-tender but not mushy. Drain immediately.

Make Paprika Butter by melting butter; stir in ½ teaspoon salt, white pepper, and paprika.

Arrange broccoli on serving platter. Pour Paprika Butter over broccoli. Serve immediately. Serves 6.

lima bean creole

2 packages (10 ounces each) frozen lima beans
6 slices bacon
¼ cup finely chopped onion
2 tablespoons chopped green pepper
½ teaspoon salt
Pepper, to taste
2 cups cooked or canned tomatoes

Cook beans as directed on package; drain.

Fry bacon; drain on absorbent paper. In 2 tablespoons bacon drippings, brown onion and green pepper. Crumble bacon. Add browned onion and green pepper, bacon, seasonings, and tomatoes to beans. Cover; simmer gently 15 minutes. Serves 6.

variations

Green bean creole. Use 2 packages (10 ounces each) frozen cut green beans instead of lima beans.

Eggplant creole. Use 1 medium-size eggplant, pared and cubed, instead of beans. Do not cook eggplant before combining with other ingredients. Increase salt to 1 teaspoon. Cook 15 to 20 minutes, until eggplant is tender.

boiled beets in yogurt

3 cups cooked or canned sliced beets
½ cup plain yogurt
1 tablespoon prepared horseradish
1 tablespoon chopped chives
1 teaspoon grated onion

Combine all ingredients in the top of a double boiler. Heat thoroughly. Season to taste; serve. Serves 4.

brussels sprouts in beer

1 pound fresh brussels sprouts
Beer (enough to cover sprouts)
½ teaspoon salt
2 tablespoons butter

Trim and wash sprouts. Place in medium-size saucepan; pour over enough beer to cover.

Bring to boil, reduce heat; simmer 20 minutes or until tender. Add more beer if needed, as liquid evaporates. Drain; add salt and butter. Serve hot. Serves 3 to 4.

fried cabbage

3 small cabbages
Pepper
1 cup flour
2 eggs, beaten
1½ cups bread crumbs
2 cups oil

Halve cabbages. Cut out cores. Cook 20 minutes in salted water. Squeeze dry; flatten out. Season with pepper. Dip in flour, beaten eggs and breadcrumbs. Fry until brown. Serves 6 to 8.

puffed cauliflower cheese

1 medium sized head of
  cauliflower
1/4 cup margarine
2 tablespoons flour
1 cup milk, or milk and
  water in which the
  cauliflower has been
  cooked

Salt
Pepper
1/4 cup fine white
  bread crumbs
3 eggs (separated)
1 cup grated cheese

Pre-heat oven to 400°F. Wash cauliflower, remove stalk end, cut into quarters; remove hard stalk. Divide into florets; cook in boiling salted water until tender. Drain.

Heat fat in pan, add flour; stir over low heat 2 minutes. Remove from heat, add milk gradually; stir until smooth. Return to heat; stir until boiling. Add salt and pepper and most of bread crumbs. Stir in egg yolks, grated cheese and cauliflower. Adjust seasoning to taste.

Beat egg whites until stiff, and fold into the mixture. Put into a greased ovenproof dish, sprinkle with the remaining breadcrumbs, and bake for about 30 minutes until well risen and brown.
Serves 4.

chinese-style cauliflower

1 head cauliflower
  florets, thinly sliced
1 teaspoon salt
1/3 cup hot water

2 tablespoons butter or
  margarine
2 tablespoons cream
Chives or parsley cut-up

Place cauliflower in heavy pan, sprinkle with salt, and add hot water.

Cook covered about 5 minutes or until slightly crisp.

Add fat and cream.

Heat for 1 or 2 minutes longer.

Garnish with cut-up chives or parsley. Serves 6.

braised celery

1 bunch celery
1/2 teaspoon salt
1/4 teaspoon pepper
2 tablespoons polyun-
  saturated margarine

1 chicken bouillon cube,
  dissolved in 1 cup
  boiling water
1 tablespoon finely
  chopped parsley

Remove green leaves from celery and cut stalks in 4-inch lengths. Arrange stalks in bottom of a small pan or heat-proof casserole. Season with salt and pepper. Dot with margarine, and pour chicken bouillon over celery. Bring the liquid to a boil, cover pan or casserole, and simmer for 30 minutes or until celery is tender.

Place on heated serving dish and sprinkle with parsley. Serves 4.

**2 1-pound cans whole
green beans**

lemon butter
**¼ cup butter
2 tablespoons lemon
juice
½ teaspoon salt
½ teaspoon dried basil
2 teaspoons dried
parsley flakes**

Drain green beans. Bring drained liquid to a boil in saucepan large enough to hold green beans horizontally when re-added to liquid. When liquid comes to a boil, reduce heat to simmer; add green beans. Simmer beans 4 minutes or until heated. Do not boil. Drain beans. Reserve liquid for soup stock.

Prepare Lemon Butter. Melt butter. Stir in lemon juice, spices, and parsley flakes.

Arrange green beans on serving platter; coat with Lemon Butter. Serve immediately. Serves 6.

note
The secret to using commercially canned vegetables is to remember the vegetables have been cooked in the canning process. Therefore, when serving canned vegetables, only reheat them.

**2 packages (10 ounces
each) frozen cut green
beans
¼ cup finely chopped
onion
¼ cup water
1 teaspoon salt
1 can (10½ ounces)
condensed cream of
mushroom soup
1 can (4 ounces)
mushroom stems and
pieces, drained,
chopped
½ cup canned french-
fried onion rings**

**green bean-
mushroom
casserole**

Cook beans and chopped onion in water with salt until beans are tender, 12 to 15 minutes. Drain.

Stir in undiluted soup and mushrooms. Pour into greased 1½-quart casserole. Top with onion rings. Cover; bake at 350° F. 30 minutes, or until mixture is heated through and top is brown. Serves 6.

Picture on opposite page: spiced green beans

corn pudding

1 tablespoon butter or
  margarine
1 tablespoon flour
1 cup scalded milk
1 teaspoon salt
1/8 teaspoon pepper
1 teaspoon sugar
1 16-ounce can cream-
  style corn
4 slightly beaten eggs

Preheat oven to 375°F. Grease 1-quart casserole.

Melt fat, blend in flour. Add milk, salt, pepper, and sugar. Add corn; heat slightly.

Blend eggs into warm milk mixture. Pour into casserole. Place casserole in pan of hot water.

Bake 1 hour or until set. Serves 6.

baked cucumbers

3 good-sized cucumbers
3 tablespoons butter
1½ tablespoons
  chopped onion
¾ cup fine dry
  bread crumbs
½ teaspoon salt
1½ teaspoons finely
  chopped parsley
1 tablespoon chopped
  celery
1 cup tomatoes cut in
  pieces

Wash cucumbers; cut in half lengthwise. Scoop out as much pulp as possible without breaking the skin.

Brown onion in fat, add other ingredients mixed with cucumber pulp. Stir constantly; cook 5 minutes, or until dry.

Place filling in cucumber shells; bake until shells are soft and mixture is brown on top. Serves 4 to 6.

corn fritters

1 1-pound can whole-
  kernel corn, drained
1 egg
½ teaspoon salt
¼ cup milk
1 cup flour
2 teaspoons baking
  powder
2 teaspoons melted
  butter or margarine
½ teaspoon sugar
Deep fat for frying

While allowing corn to drain, mix egg, salt, milk, flour, baking powder, melted butter, and sugar. Stir with a wooden spoon. Add drained corn. After corn is mixed in allow to sit 5 minutes.

Drop mixture by teaspoonfuls into hot fat. Cook until puffy and golden brown, drain on paper; transfer to a warmed platter. Serves 4 to 6.

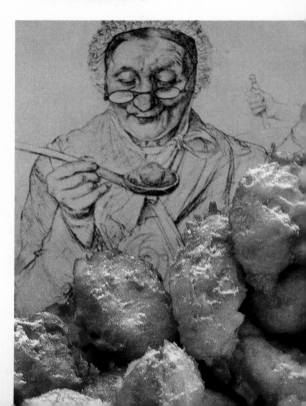

corn fritters

stuffed eggplant

2 small eggplants (about
  ¾ pound each)
3 tablespoons olive oil
2 tablespoons butter
2 medium onions, thinly
  sliced
1 pound tomatoes,
  peeled, seeded, and
  chopped
2 cloves garlic
½ teaspoon salt
1 bay leaf
1 2-inch stick of
  cinnamon
¼ teaspoon pepper
½ cup finely chopped
  parsley
8 black olives
8 anchovy fillets

Remove stems and cap from eggplants. Heat olive oil in large
skillet, add eggplants. Cook over medium-high heat 5 minutes.
Remove from pan. Cut in half lengthwise. Carefully scoop out
pulp, leaving a thin shell. Chop eggplant pulp coarsely.

Heat butter in same skillet. Add onions; cook until golden. Add
tomatoes and eggplant pulp; cook 10 minutes. Crush garlic cloves
with salt. Add to tomato mixture. Add bay leaf, cinnamon stick,
pepper, and parsley; cook 10 more minutes.

Fill eggplant shells with mixture. Garnish each shell with 2 olives
and 2 anchovy fillets. Bake at 375°F 10 minutes; serve. Serves 4.

stuffed eggplant

red cabbage

red cabbage

1 large head red
  cabbage
2 tablespoons bacon fat
  or oil
½ cup red wine
3 tablespoons red
  currant jelly

1 teaspoon salt
Dash of white pepper
Pinch of powdered
  cloves
1 tablespoon sugar

Wash, shred, and drain red cabbage.

Heat bacon fat or oil in large pot. Add cabbage; heat 5 minutes.
Add red wine, currant jelly, salt, pepper, cloves, and sugar. Mix
very well.

Continue to stir a few minutes until all flavors are absorbed. Cover;
cook cabbage over low heat 25 minutes. Serve cabbage hot.
Serves 6 to 8.

46

glazed carrots

10 to 12 medium carrots
4 tablespoons butter
**½ teaspoon salt and
  pepper**
2 tablespoons sugar
2 tablespoons parsley

Peel carrots; cut into 2-inch cylinders. Bring all ingredients, except parsley, to a boil over moderate heat. Cover; simmer over low heat. Shake skillet occasionally to roll carrots about. If liquid cooks away too fast, add more water.

In 20 to 30 minutes carrots should be tender and liquid should be a brown, syrupy glaze. If liquid is not reduced enough, remove carrots and boil liquid down. Roll carrots in glaze, sprinkle with parsley. Serves 4 to 5.

note
Small onions can be cooked the same way.

eggplant parmesan

1 medium eggplant
3 cups bread crumbs
**1 egg, slightly beaten
  with**
2 tablespoons water

3 cups tomato sauce
2 cups grated cheese
**3 tablespoons Parmesan
  cheese**
Oil

Peel eggplant and slice into about ¼-inch slices. Dip eggplant into egg–water mixture, then into crumbs. (You can season bread crumbs with 1 tablespoon oregano if you like.)

Sauté in an oiled frying pan until brown. When done, drain on absorbent paper; set aside. Repeat with rest of eggplant slices. In a baking pan put a layer of tomato sauce, a layer of eggplant, and layer of cheese. Sprinkle with Parmesan cheese; repeat process until eggplant is all used. Finish with a layer of cheese. Put in a 400° oven until cheese is melted. Serves 4.

eggplant-tomato casserole

1 large onion, chopped
**2 small eggplants,
  peeled and diced**
**¼ cup butter or
  margarine**
**1 28-ounce can
  tomatoes, drained**
1 teaspoon salt
⅛ teaspoon pepper
¼ cup corn flake crumbs

Preheat oven to 350°F.

Cook onion and eggplant in fat until golden brown. Add tomatoes, salt, and pepper. Mix thoroughly. Pour into casserole; top with crumbs.

Bake 30 minutes. Serves 6.

vegetable in cream sauce

2 tablespoons fat
  (margarine or butter)
2 tablespoons flour
1 cup fluid milk
Salt and pepper to taste

3 cups drained, cooked
  or canned vegetable
  (such as carrots, peas,
  green beans, lima
  beans, or spinach)

Heat fat, stir in flour.

Add milk slowly, stirring until smooth. Cook and stir until mixture is thickened.

Add salt and pepper and vegetable. Heat. Serves 6.

variations

Vegetable in butter sauce. Use recipe for Vegetable in Cream Sauce. Use 1 cup liquid from the vegetable in place of milk or use part vegetable liquid and part milk.

Vegetable in cheese sauce. Use recipe for Vegetable in Cream Sauce. Add ¾ cup finely cut-up cheese to sauce. Stir over low heat until cheese melts.

mexican rice

3 tablespoons vegetable
  oil
½ cup chopped onion
1 clove garlic, minced
1 cup raw long-grain rice
¼ cup chopped red
  pepper
½ teaspoon salt
Dash of cayenne pepper
2 cups boiling water
2 teaspoons chicken
  broth granules
¾ cup frozen peas and
  carrots, thawed
1 small tomato, peeled,
  seeded, and chopped
  (about ⅓ cup)

Heat oil in heavy frypan over medium heat. Add onion, garlic, rice, and red pepper; sauté until onion is limp and rice is opaque. Add salt, cayenne pepper, boiling water, and chicken broth granules.

Cover; cook 20 minutes or until liquid is absorbed. Add peas and carrots and tomato. Serve rice immediately. Serves 4 to 6.

stuffed green peppers

3 large green peppers
2 teaspoons salt
Boiling water
1 pound ground beef
1½ cups cooked rice
2 tablespoons finely
 chopped celery

2 tablespoons finely
 chopped onion
¼ cup chili sauce
2 teaspoons salt
¼ teaspoon pepper
1 egg
2 tablespoons shredded
 cheddar cheese

Halve peppers lengthwise; remove stems, seeds, and membranes. Add 2 teaspoons salt to enough boiling water to cover peppers; boil peppers 5 minutes. Drain.

Combine other ingredients except cheese; mix well. Fill pepper halves with mixture; place in ½ inch hot water in a baking pan.

Bake uncovered at 350° F 45 to 55 minutes. Sprinkle cheese over peppers; bake 5 minutes longer, or just until cheese melts. Serves 6.

potato-garlic scallop

1 clove garlic
4 tablespoons butter
4 cups thinly sliced
 potatoes (¼ inch
 thick)
1 cup grated Swiss
 cheese
1½ cups hot milk
1 teaspoon salt
⅛ teaspoon pepper

Cut garlic in half; rub over inside of 2-quart baking dish. Using 1 tablespoon butter, thoroughly grease casserole. Spread half of potatoes in dish. Cover with half of cheese. Add remaining potatoes; top with cheese.

Mix milk, salt, and pepper. Pour over potatoes. Dot with remaining 3 tablespoons butter. Bake in preheated 375°F oven 45 to 60 minutes. Reduce heat or add more milk if potatoes become dry before they are tender. When done, the top should be nicely browned. Serves 4 to 6.

potato balls

2 cups mashed potatoes
1 egg with 2 tablespoons
 water
Crushed cornflakes
Fat for deep frying

Shape mashed potatoes into ice-cream-scoop balls. Roll each ball in egg mixture, then in crushed cornflakes.

Heat fat in medium-size skillet. Fry balls in deep fat until nicely browned all over.

Put on a warming platter until all are cooked. Serves 4 to 6.

49

mushroom pie

pastry for an 8 inch two-
  crust pie
1 cup milk
1 blade mace
1 bay leaf
6 peppercorns
3 tablespoons butter or
  margarine
1 small onion, peeled
  and sliced thinly
2 cups sliced
  mushrooms
3 tablespoons flour
2 tablespoons heavy
  cream
1 egg yolk
1 egg

Pre-heat oven to 400°F. Line an 8- inch pie plate with about ⅔ of pastry.

Put milk into pan, add mace, bay leaf and peppercorns. Place over very low heat to infuse. Strain off milk; discard flavorings.

Heat half the butter in pan, add onion; sauté until soft but not colored. Add mushrooms, increase heat a little. Cook for 2 to 3 minutes, stirring occasionally. Add remaining butter; stir in flour. Add milk gradually, stir until boiling; remove from heat. Add cream, egg yolk and seasoning. Let cool a little; put into pastry shell.

Roll out remaining pastry; cut into thin strips. Arrange in lattice forms over pie, pressing ends of strips well down onto edge of pastry. Brush with beaten egg, bake about 30 to 35 minutes; serve with a green salad. Serves 4.

mushrooms in cream sauce

1½ to 2 pounds fresh
  mushrooms
¼ pound bacon, diced
¼ cup butter or
  margarine
2 large onions, diced
1 cup white wine
½ teaspoon salt
¼ teaspoon pepper
¼ teaspoon paprika
Pinch of nutmeg
Pinch of mace
1 cup heavy cream
Juice of ½ lemon
2 sprigs parsley

Clean mushrooms; slice in half if large. Pat dry.

Fry bacon in a large pan until lightly browned. Remove from pan; reserve. Add butter to pan drippings. Add onions; sauté until lightly browned. Add mushrooms; cook until tender, stirring often. Stir in wine, salt, pepper, paprika, nutmeg, and mace. Cover frypan; cook over low heat 15 minutes.

Off the heat, add the cooked bacon, cream, and lemon juice. Reheat until just warm. Do not let mixture boil.

Garnish with parsley; serve with noodles or dumplings. Serves 4 to 6.

green peas bonne femme

green peas bonne femme

¼ pound Canadian bacon, cut in 1-inch pieces	Inner leaves of lettuce head
1 tablespoon margarine	½ cup water
3 cups fresh green peas	½ teaspoon salt
6 small white onions, peeled	¼ teaspoon pepper
	½ teaspoon sugar
	1 tablespoon finely chopped parsley

Fry bacon in margarine until lightly browned. Add peas, onions, lettuce, water, salt, pepper, and sugar. Cover; cook 10 to 15 minutes or until peas are tender.

When peas are done, drain remaining liquid. Sprinkle with parsley before serving. Serves 6.

stuffed baked tomatoes

4 large tomatoes
¼ cup butter
½ cup finely chopped
onions
½ cup tomato centers
(from above tomatoes)

½ teaspoon salt
¼ teaspoon black
pepper
¼ teaspoon oregano
2 cups bread crumbs
1 bunch parsley

stuffed baked tomatoes

Thoroughly wash tomatoes. Dry on a paper towel. With a sharp knife, remove tops from tomatoes. Save tomato tops for later use. Scoop centers from tomatoes; reserve ½ cup for later use.

Heat butter in medium-size skillet. Add onions; cook until tender. Add ½ cup tomato centers to onions; cook until tomato pieces are mushy.

Combine spices and bread crumbs. Add cooked vegetables and butter. Work bread and vegetables with your hands until well-combined and stuffing mix has formed. If stuffing mix is too dry, add more melted butter.

Fill tomato cavities with stuffing mixture. Place tomatoes close together in a slightly greased baking pan. If tomatoes are small enough, they can be baked in a greased muffin tin. Replace tomato tops. Bake tomatoes in 350°F oven 30 minutes or until fork-tender.

Carefully arrange tomatoes on serving platter. Garnish with fresh parsley. Serves 4.

provincial vegetable casserole

1 medium eggplant
1 tablespoon salt
¼ cup olive or vegetable oil
2 large onions, sliced
3 cloves garlic, crushed
1 medium red pepper (optional), cored and cut into cubes
1 medium green pepper, cored and cut into cubes
4 medium zucchini, sliced ¾ inch thick
3 medium tomatoes, peeled, seeded, and cut into coarse cubes
¼ teaspoon salt
Freshly ground pepper to taste
¼ teaspoon thyme
¼ teaspoon oregano
1 bay leaf
2 tablespoons chopped parsley

Cut eggplant into ½-inch-thick slices, then into chunks. Sprinkle with 1 tablespoon salt; let stand 30 minutes. Dry thoroughly after standing.

Heat oil in large frying pan. Sauté onions and garlic 2 minutes. Add red and green peppers; cook 2 minutes more. Add eggplant; brown lightly on both sides (about 3 minutes). Add zucchini, tomatoes, and seasonings, except parsley. Simmer gently, un-covered, 30 to 40 minutes, until all vegetables are just tender. Baste vegetables often; do not scorch. Cover; reduce heat if necessary. Remove bay leaf; chill.

Garnish casserole with parsley. Serve. May be served hot or cold. Serves 8 to 10.

provincial vegetable casserole

sweet-and-sour yams and pineapple

sweet-and-sour yams and pineapple

1 20-ounce can sliced pineapple; drain and reserve syrup
1 tablespoon cornstarch
¼ teaspoon salt
3 tablespoons fresh lemon juice
2 1-pound cans of yams, drained
Oil
4 scallions, sliced
1 small green pepper, cut into small chunks
½ cup celery, sliced diagonally

Drain pineapple; reserve syrup. In saucepan, combine reserved syrup, cornstarch and salt. Blend well. Bring to a boil over medium heat. Cook until thickened, stirring constantly. Stir in the lemon juice. Arrange pineapple and yams in casserole and pour the sauce over mixture. Bake, covered, in a 350°F oven for about 30 minutes or until hot. In small amount of oil in skillet, sauté scallions, green pepper chunks and celery until just tender, but still crisp. Stir carefully into yam mixture. Serve immediately. Serves 8.

cauliflower with water chestnuts and mushrooms

1 small cauliflower
2 tablespoons oil
8 mushrooms, sliced
1 cup hot chicken broth
¼ cup sliced water chestnuts
2 tablespoons soy sauce
½ teaspoon monosodium glutamate
Salt to taste
1 tablespoon cornstarch mixed with cold water

Trim and wash cauliflower. Break into florets. If florets are large, slice.

Heat oil in pan; gently sauté cauliflower. Add sliced mushrooms; sauté about 30 seconds. Add chicken broth, sliced water chestnuts, soy sauce, and seasonings. Bring mixture to a boil, cover; simmer until cauliflower is just tender, i.e. still crunchy.

Mix cornstarch with enough cold water to make a smooth paste; slowly add to cauliflower mixture, stirring constantly until thickened. Serves 4.

broiled tomatoes

4 medium tomatoes

seasoned butter
¼ cup butter
1 teaspoon garlic salt
**¼ teaspoon white
   pepper**
¼ teaspoon dry mustard

Wash tomatoes. Place upside down on broiler pan. With a sharp knife, slash skins of tomatoes in an "X" design.

Make Seasoned Butter. Melt butter; stir in garlic salt, white pepper, and dry mustard.

Brush tomatoes with Seasoned Butter. Place broiling pan in farthest slot from flame. Broil tomatoes 2 minutes. Remove tomatoes from broiler; baste again with Seasoned Butter. Return to broiler; continue to broil 3 minutes. Serves 4.

fried green tomatoes

**4 medium green
   tomatoes, sliced ½
   inch thick**
1 teaspoon salt
½ teaspoon pepper
1 teaspoon dillweed
1 cup cornmeal
Fat for frying

Wash and prepare tomatoes— these must be green.

Mix seasonings with cornmeal in a pie plate. Batter each tomato slice, being sure both sides are coated.

Heat fat in medium skillet; cook tomatoes until brown on both sides. Drain on paper towels. Serves 4 to 6.

tomatoes rockefeller

**3 large tomatoes, cut in
   half and seeds
   removed**
**2 tablespoons finely
   chopped onion**
**1 tablespoon finely
   chopped parsley**
**2 tablespoons
   margarine**

**½ cup chopped cooked
   spinach, drained well**
¼ teaspoon salt
⅛ teaspoon pepper
¼ teaspoon paprika
**2 tablespoons bread
   crumbs**

Place tomatoes in a shallow baking dish, cut side up.

Mix the rest of ingredients except bread crumbs. Divide and spread evenly over tomatoes. Top with crumbs. Bake in a preheated 375°F oven 15 minutes or until crumbs are toasted and tomato is heated. Serves 6.

turnips au gratin

2 tablespoons butter or
  margarine
2 tablespoons flour
¼ teaspoon salt
1 cup milk

3 cups diced turnips,
  cooked
1 cup or 4 ounces
  shredded, process
  cheddar cheese

Preheat oven to 375°F.

Melt fat in a saucepan. Stir in flour and salt until smooth. Add milk slowly while stirring rapidly to prevent lumping. Bring mixture to a boil, stirring constantly.

Gently mix white sauce and turnips; pour into baking dish. Sprinkle with cheese. Bake about 20 minutes or until cheese melts. Serves 6.

variation
Celery au gratin. Use cooked, sliced celery in place of turnips.

glazed turnips

2 pounds turnips, peeled
  and quartered
2 tablespoons vegetable
  oil
1 to 1½ cups beef
  bouillon

1 tablespoon margarine
3 tablespoons sugar
2 tablespoons minced
  parsley

Blanch turnips in boiling salted water to cover 5 minutes. Drain; pat dry with paper towels.

Sauté turnips in hot oil 3 minutes to lightly brown. Pour in bouillon to barely cover. Add margarine and sugar. Cover; boil slowly 20 to 30 minutes or until turnips are just tender. Uncover; boil liquid down to reduce to a thick syrup. Gently top turnips and coat with glaze.

Place in a vegetable dish or around a roast; sprinkle with parsley. Serves 6.

chinese fried vegetables

Oil for cooking
½ cup celery, sliced
  diagonally
4 ounces bamboo shoots
4 ounces water
  chestnuts, sliced

3 scallions, sliced into
  1-inch pieces
½ cup fresh mushrooms
1 cup bean sprouts,
  fresh or canned
Soy sauce to taste

Heat oil in skillet or wok. Add celery, bamboo shoots and water chestnuts. Stir-fry 2 minutes. Add scallions, mushrooms and bean sprouts; stir-fry 1 minute or until heated through. Sprinkle with soy sauce to taste; serve immediately. Serves 2.

delicious spinach

1 pound fresh spinach, washed and cut into 2-inch pieces
2 tablespoons oil
Salt to taste
1 small can bamboo shoots
8 fresh mushrooms, sliced
¼ cup chicken broth

Wash and cut spinach into pieces. Heat oil in skillet or wok. Add salt and spinach; stir-fry 2 minutes.

Add bamboo shoots, mushrooms, and chicken broth. Mix, cover; simmer about 2 minutes, or until heated through. Serves 2.

stuffed squash

3 tablespoons oil
1 onion
¾ pound chopped cooked meat
1 cup chopped mushrooms
1 tablespoon flour
1 cup gravy (or tomato sauce)
1 tablespoon soy or Worcestershire sauce
1 tablespoon mixed herbs
¼ cup leftover peas, beans, carrots, corn or rice
1 summer squash, about 2 pounds
3 tablespoons dried white bread crumbs
A little melted butter
2 tablespoons chopped parsley

Pre-heat oven to 375°F. Heat oil; cook chopped onion until golden brown. Add chopped meat and mushrooms, cook 2 minutes. Sprinkle with flour; mix in. Add enough gravy (or tomato sauce) to moisten, but do not make too soft. Add soy or Worcestershire sauce, mixed herbs and vegetables or rice.

Cut squash in half lengthwise; remove seeds, or cut into 1½ inch thick rings, remove seeds. Boil squash 5 minutes; drain. Put in a buttered ovenproof dish; fill with meat mixture.

Sprinkle with dried white bread crumbs. Pour over a little melted butter. Pour remaining gravy round squash. Cook in oven about 35 to 50 minutes, according to thickness of squash. Test with skewer. When tender sprinkle with chopped parsley. Serves 4 to 6.

squash and tomatoes

3 medium-size or 6 small zucchini or yellow summer squash
1 small onion
2 slices bread
2 cups fresh or canned tomatoes
½ teaspoon salt
Pepper to taste

Slice squash. Chop onion. Cut up bread.

Mix all ingredients in a saucepan. Cover; boil gently about 30 minutes until squash is tender and flavors are blended.

Add salt and pepper. Serves 6.

stuffed zucchini

6 medium zucchini
2 tablespoons margarine
½ cup chopped onion
1 cup chopped tomato
1 cup (6 ounces)
   shredded cheddar
   cheese
4 slices of crisply
   cooked bacon,
   crumbled or bacon
   bits
1 teaspoon salt
¼ teaspoon poultry
   seasoning
Dash of pepper

Heat oven to 350°F. Trim ends of zucchini; cook in boiling water 5 to 8 minutes. Drain zucchini; cut in half, lengthwise. Scoop out centers; chop pulp.

Cook onion in margarine until tender. Mix chopped zucchini, chopped tomato, onion, cheese and bacon with seasoning. Place in hollowed zucchini; arrange in baking pan. Bake at 350°F 30 minutes. Serves 6.

zucchini italian

2 tablespoons butter or
   shortening
1 onion, sliced into rings
1 pound zucchini, sliced
   (2 to 3 cups)
1 cup diced fresh
   tomatoes
1 teaspoon salt
Dash of pepper
1 teaspoon dillweed

Heat butter in medium skillet. Use skillet with its own top. Cook onion rings in butter until yellow. Add zucchini, tomatoes, salt, pepper, and dillweed. Cover; lower heat to simmer. Cook from 10 to 15 minutes, until vegetables are tender.

If you want this for company and want to make it ahead, put the cooked vegetables in a casserole dish and sprinkle with grated cheese. Just before serving, put into moderate oven for 5 minutes or until cheese has browned. Serves 4.

spinach casserole

spinach casserole

2 pounds spinach	4 eggs
1 tablespoon olive oil	¼ cup heavy cream
1 clove garlic, minced	Butter to grease dish
½ teaspoon salt	2 tablespoons dried
⅛ teaspoon pepper	bread crumbs
⅛ teaspoon ground	(packaged)
nutmeg	1 tablespoon butter

Thoroughly wash spinach; drain. Heat oil in large Dutch oven or saucepan. Add garlic; cook 1 minute. Add spinach; cover; steam 3 minutes. Season with salt, pepper, and nutmeg.

In small bowl beat eggs and cream until well-blended. Stir in spinach. Grease ovenproof dish with butter; spoon in spinach mixture.

Sprinkle with bread crumbs; dot with butter. Place in preheated 425°F oven. Bake spinach about 15 minutes or until lightly browned. Serves 6 to 8.

rice and vegetable ring

1 cup rice	Salt
½ pound mushrooms	Paprika
4 tablespoons margarine	1 pound green beans or
4 tablespoons stock or	1 head of cauliflower
water	

Cook rice in boiling salted water. Drain.

Chop mushrooms; sauté 2 to 3 minutes in 2 tablespoons of fat. Add stock; combine with rice. Season to taste with salt and paprika.

Press rice mixture firmly into a greased 7-inch ring mold. let stand about 5 minutes. Turn out on a platter; keep warm.

Cook vegetable while rice is cooking. If cauliflower is used, divide into florets. Pile vegetable into center of mold; dot with remaining margarine. Serves 6.

note
Almost any vegetable can be used to fill center of this ring. Green beans or cauliflower, when plentiful, are particularly suitable.

59

potato pancakes with chives

2 tablespoons chopped
   chives
4 medium baked
   potatoes, grated
2 teaspoons salt
Several twists of freshly
   ground black pepper

1 tablespoon flour
2 tablespoons butter or
   margarine
2 tablespoons vegetable
   oil

Chop chives first; set aside.

Peel and grate potatoes coarsely into a large mixing bowl. Potatoes will accumulate potato water. Do not drain. Mix in chopped chives, salt, and pepper. Work as quickly as you can, so that potatoes do not turn brown. Add flour, mixing well.

Melt shortening in a large skillet. Drop potato mixture by spoonfuls into hot fat. The 3-inch pancakes will take about 3 minutes a side to become crisp and golden. Serve piping hot. Serves 4.

fried zucchini

3 to 4 large zucchini,
   sliced into rounds
1 egg
1 tablespoon milk
3 tablespoons flour
1 teaspoon salt
1 teaspoon garlic salt
Deep fat for frying

Wash and slice zucchini into rounds about ¼ inch thick. Set aside.

Combine egg, milk, flour, salt, and garlic salt in a bowl. Mix well to form batter. Dip each zucchini round into batter; fry in deep fat. Batter zucchini as you are ready to fry it, so each piece is coated. Fry until crisp and golden brown. Drain on paper towels. Serve hot. Serves 4 to 6.

zucchini and cheese bake

2 medium zucchini
   squashes, sliced
1 small onion, chopped
2 tablespoons vegetable
   oil
½ pound cottage cheese
½ teaspoon basil
2 tablespoons Parmesan
   cheese

Sauté zucchini and onion in hot oil. Drain.

Puree cottage cheese and basil in a blender.

Alternate layers of cheese and zucchini in a greased ovenproof casserole dish. Sprinkle Parmesan cheese on top. Bake uncovered at 350°F 20 to 25 minutes. Serves 4.

SALAD DRESSINGS

bleu or roquefort cheese dressing

4 ounces bleu or
   Roquefort cheese,
   crumbled
1 cup sour cream
1 teaspoon lemon juice

1 teaspoon sugar
1 teaspoon instant
   minced onion
½ teaspoon salt

Mix all ingredients well.

Chill, preferably overnight, to allow flavors to blend. Use within a week. About 1½ cups dressing.

french dressing

2 tablespoons white
   wine vinegar
Salt
Freshly ground black
   pepper
6 to 8 tablespoons olive
   oil

Mix vinegar with salt and pepper to taste. Add oil; beat with a fork until mixture thickens. About ½ cup dressing.

note
For a slightly thicker dressing, add an ice cube. Stir 1 to 2 minutes longer, then remove ice cube.

variations
Tarragon dressing. Add 1 teaspoon chopped fresh tarragon leaves.

Curry dressing. Add ½ teaspoon curry powder and 1 teaspoon finely chopped shallots.

Caper dressing. Add 1 teaspoon chopped capers, ½ clove garlic, finely crushed, and a little anchovy paste.

Roquefort dressing. Add 3 tablespoons crumbled Roquefort cheese; blend well. Chill before serving.

½ cup sugar
1 tablespoon flour
1 egg
3 tablespoons lemon
   juice
¾ cup pineapple juice

Mix all ingredients.

Cook over low heat, stirring constantly, until mixture is thick and clear. Chill. About 1¼ cups dressing.

variation
Honey-lime salad dressing. Use ½ cup honey and ¼ cup lime juice in place of sugar and lemon juice. Reduce pineapple juice to ½ cup.

1 cup mayonnaise
1 clove garlic, crushed
¼ cup finely chopped
   parsley
2 tablespoons chopped
   chives
1 tablespoon lemon
   juice

1 tablespoon tarragon
   vinegar
½ teaspoon salt, black
   pepper
2 teaspoons anchovy
   paste
2 tablespoons cream

Combine all ingredients; stir until dressing is smooth. Makes about 2 cups dressing.

note
For all seafood salads

2 egg yolks
½ teaspoon salt
¼ teaspoon dry mustard
1½ teaspoons wine
   vinegar
1 cup olive oil
½ teaspoon lemon juice

Rinse a bowl with hot water; dry well. Put in egg yolks, salt and mustard and 1 teaspoon vinegar. Beat vigorously or at low speed with electric mixer.

Add half the oil, drop by drop, then remaining vinegar. Beat in rest of oil in a steady stream.

Add lemon juice. Makes about 1 cup.

note
If mayonnaise curdles, break an egg yolk into a clean basin; gradually beat curdled mixture into it.

Index

63